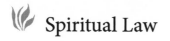 Spiritual Law

SWEDENBORG'S

DIVINE PROVIDENCE

Joanna V. Hill

ROCK POINT PRESS
Santa Fe, New Mexico

For my lovely daughter
Louisa, *the light of my life*

Rock Point Press
7 Avenida Vista Grande
Suite B7-403
Santa Fe, New Mexico 87508
www.rockpointpress.com

Printed in Canada
ISBN 978-0-9912516-0-5
Library of Congress Control Number: 2014912635

Cover photograph by Joanna V. Hill

 Contents

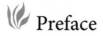 Preface

Emanuel Swedenborg was an eighteenth-century Swedish scientist, nobleman, philosopher, and theologian who wrote over thirty theological books after a career of writing scientific works. These later books are based on his experiences in the heavenly realms after he had an awakening experience and his spiritual eyes were opened.

Divine Providence, the focus of this book and one of his later works, is a compilation of many of the insights explained in his earlier theological works, but this time he condensed and presented them with greater clarity and focus. The ideas contained within this work are relevant to all spiritual and religious paths, even though Swedenborg speaks from a Christian perspective.

Although most people are not aware of the books written by Emanuel Swedenborg, they have made unique contributions to great thinkers, both past and present. Through the years, famous writers, philosophers, poets, theologians, and scholars have been influenced by his wisdom and insights, including such people as C. G. Jung, Jorge Luis Borges, Czeslaw Milosz, Ralph Waldo Emerson, Helen Keller, D. T. Suzuki, Henry Corbin, and William Blake. In addition to the contributions that his writings have made on intellectual and spiritual development in the past, it is also important to see how this information is particularly useful in our modern world.

Increasingly, people are seeking to understand the deep mysteries of the cosmos, how the world operates, and by what principles. Many individuals are exploring different pathways to the sacred in the endless varieties of spiritual paths, books, and disciplines that are available today. It is in the recognition of this spiritual hunger for solid insights that this presentation of his work was prepared.

This book is a derivative work taken from the text written by Emanuel Swedenborg and published in Amsterdam in 1764 in Latin, the scholarly language of the eighteenth century. The translated title of the original work is *Angelic Wisdom Regarding Divine Providence*. This book is not meant to be a substitute for the complete work but offers an approach to understand some of its basic concepts, and may lead a reader to investigate these ideas in the original.

The story begins in 1688 when Emanuel Swedenborg was born in Stockholm, Sweden, the son of a Lutheran bishop. He lived until 1772 and in the interim traveled and studied at the university in Uppsala, Sweden, and also in England, France, Holland, and Germany. His first fields of study were mathematics and astronomy, and later metallurgy and geology. He became assessor on the Board of Mines in Sweden and wrote many scientific treatises on various topics in the physical sciences.

Later he explored areas relating to anatomy and the workings of the brain, as well as psychology, and even recorded his dreams in an attempt to understand their deepest meaning. His scientific explorations continued as he searched for the source of the soul within the human body, an endeavor that culminated in a series of visions and spiritual awakenings that revealed deep mysteries of the order of the universe, the afterlife, and the inner meaning of scripture. As a result of these spiritual experiences, he turned his full attention to theological writing in 1745 and spent the next twenty-seven years recording the insights and information he received from the spiritual world.

This body of knowledge, now encompassing thirty volumes, is referred to as the writings of Emanuel Swedenborg. Contained within them are explanations of a symbolic meaning of scripture, descriptions of heaven and heavenly communities, a new under-standing of the life of Christ, a history of the evolution of world religions, and of insights into attaining spiritual awareness and salvation.

Throughout the writings comes a clear message of a loving God who is leading us to heaven. For one who is searching for genuine truth and wisdom, reading Swedenborg's writings is like having a veil lifted. We can still choose which path to take, but with the clarity of having an informed guide. The information that Swedenborg reveals makes us aware of the heavenly influ-ence that surrounds us at all times and points us constantly to a life of love and wisdom, leading to heaven.

The ideas that are expressed may seem old fashioned to some. I have not taken great efforts to disguise Swedenborg's concept of God by naming it otherwise, such as the Creative Life Force or the Ultimate Reality. Nor have I chosen to delete all references to the idea of good and evil as a creative tension that exists in our lives. The concept of salvation may seem scary or judgmental to some, but it can also provide a sense of liberation and freedom for those who are deeply, sincerely searching for the truth.

The ideas presented here and in other books by Swedenborg envision a new view of Christianity, and his writings address and clarify misunderstandings that have hindered the full expression of Christian faith. The particular area that we will focus on in this book is learning the spiritual laws by which God governs and interacts with our physical world.

The ideas Swedenborg conveys might be interesting and accessible to people who have thought about such things as near-death experience, life after death, the existence of angels, spiritual growth, and taking responsibility for their actions. The truth, as it turns out, is deceptively simple no matter how complicated its explanations. I have tried to take Swedenborgian concepts and state them in ways that are understandable and clear.

People coming from varied paths or religious backgrounds are searching for the truth to which all paths lead—in this world or the next. The greatest success for this book would be that it is a step along the way, that it may lead you to a serious, in-depth inquiry into the nature of transformation and spiritual growth. I would also hope that it might give you some tools with which to work in order that your life unfold according to your deepest longings. The key to spiritual transformation is building on a strong foundation of wisdom. Within Swedenborg's insights, you will find many wise teachings and loving insights that may be useful for building a spiritual home.

—JOANNA V. HILL

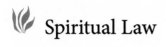 Spiritual Law

The Way God Governs the World

The way that God governs the world and the people who live here can be described as spiritual law or an ordering of the universe, also known as Divine providence. These laws address the higher aspects and development of a person much like natural laws, such as gravity, deal with the physical world. If we wish to learn how to function as loving and wise human beings, it would be beneficial to learn what these spiritual laws are so that we can develop into the type of people we choose to be.

The way that God governs is through Divine love and wisdom, or perfect love and perfect wisdom. These aspects contain the fullest sense of what the words "love" and "wisdom" could possibly encompass, which actually are much beyond our comprehension. They are contained within the creative force of the universe and are unified within the Creator. Symbolically, we can think of Divine love as heat and Divine wisdom as light. Just as the sun contains both heat and light, so does God contain and project both love and wisdom.

Although people can exist on this earth in a divided state, in life after death, or heaven, they cannot. Thus we see people who have good intentions, but make foolish or destructive choices for any number of reasons. Or there are those who know from their religion or readings what is right and true, but they act out of evil intentions or hypocritical ways. These two types of people—one with love, but no wisdom; the other with wisdom, but no love—are split. As a result, what they can do in their endeavors will be very limited and not of much use as they are divided within themselves.

The basic purpose of God's governance through Divine

providence is to protect the unity of love and wisdom. Divine order is, in fact, this unity, and spiritual law exists to make and sustain this connection. We all have within us the capacity for good and truth or evil and falsity. Being aware of Divine providence helps us learn to choose with understanding which path to follow. Even evil exists for the purpose of promoting this unification of good loves and true ideas by creating equilibrium, providing a contrast, and pointing out the areas of our lives that need attention. This works in the spiritual world as in the natural—just as one who has been cold more greatly appreciates the heat, so the experience of meanness and injustice can promote an appreciation of kindness and truth.

The creation of the world came about as a result of this Divine love through Divine wisdom; it was not created from nothingness but from God. Signs of this wisdom are evident in such creations as a seed from which grows a beautiful tree. There are several ways to evaluate natural phenomena: first instinctively, then rationally, and then spiritually. If we can look at examples of physical world first from a physical, then scientific, then transcendent perspective, we begin to sense the connection, wonder, and awe of all of creation. This creative life force exists within all living things and is evidence of Divine influence.

The union of love and wisdom within God is reflected in each human being and in every creation. There is an emanation from God to all of creation—from the highest and most pure energy descending by degrees through the levels of material creation. Thus, the more closely one is governed by this union of love and wisdom, the more closely a person reflects the image and likeness of God. Through the spiritual law of Divine providence, God works to restore this marriage of good loves and true ideas in all humans.

The marriage of good and truth, or love and wisdom, or intention and understanding, can only take place if there is a union of the two. One is good only to the extent that there is connection with truth, just as one is true only if there is unity with good. Anything else only "seems" to be good, just as gold covering rotten wood would seem to be beautiful. At its core, it is rotten. Hypocrites may speak nice words externally, but not with sincerity; in fact, they can be masking jealousy, meanness, and lies. The words sound good, but are not loving and honest.

In this world, one can be in this divided state, but it is ultimately impossible in heaven to serve two masters, and thus be driven in two different directions. On earth people can entertain both good and evil—and this is a sign that they have not looked to a higher presence in their lives. To be reformed or spiritually transformed, and thus unified, one must turn to good and truth as a choice, as a way of living life. If people examine their intentions and actions and determine some are evil, they can choose to stop for the simple reason that this behavior goes against loving God. This process, called *spiritual transformation* or *regeneration*, will restore the joining of good and truth and help one to express the loving wisdom of our Creator. The laws of providence exist to promote this unification and, thus, the ultimate elevation of human beings to a higher state of consciousness.

This process of uniting good and truth connects a person to God. A part of this effort involves facing trials or temptations while on earth, which creates tension that exists between good and evil in every person's life. From the equilibrium caused by the tension between the two, in freedom, one can choose which path to follow.

We may be dealing with feelings of greed or desires to

cause the suffering of others, or any number of negative intentions. These incidents can offer a person the opportunity to face temptations and, by fighting against these evil inclinations, be reformed or purified. Therefore a useful purpose for evil is to help people see the consequences of making selfish or destructive decisions, which provides them with the possiblity of doing otherwise. Ultimately, evil exists to allow people to see that it as a separation from the spiritual marriage of love and wisdom, both of which emanate from God.

✿ Heaven as the Ultimate Goal

God created the universe for the purpose of creating a heaven, or eternal happiness, for people who have become or are becoming angels. Just as people are created in the image and likeness of God and, as image corresponds to God's wisdom and likeness to Divine love, the unity of the two creates a Divine marriage, which is heaven. Those who live in heaven are angels.

The nature of heaven is a reciprocal connection of angels with God. One of the qualities of the spiritual world is that this connection, also called *conjunction*, is brought about by heartfelt contemplation. By thinking of something with affection, the object of concentration actually appears. This is characteristic of the spiritual world, not the natural world, since the natural world is limited by space and time. God's love flows into the affections of the angels, and then these affections go into their perceptions and thoughts, which they then turn to love of God. This cycle of love to thought and thought to love is called the *cycle of life in heaven*. This is how God exists with the angels, not as a king among the people, but as part of this conjunction of love and thoughts.

In a similar way, human beings are formed so that they have the capacity to become more and more closely connected to God by evolving through levels of spiritual development. The first level is the natural state whose highest accomplishment is rational thought and understanding. A person can advance to the next level, the spiritual, by living according to Divine truths, or spiritual law. The third level is the truly heavenly, which reflects a life devoted to loving God or the love of doing good. As one progresses, one becomes more closely conjoined to God in the process.

People's lives are ruled by their loves or their fundamental motivations, which involve not only acting on these passions, but also thinking about them and deriving pleasure from this contemplation. As discussed earlier, God's love flows into a person's loves and then into their perceptions and thoughts. If a person's loves are dominated by evil flowing into thoughts of false, incorrect, or confused ideas, this closes the door through which God's love can flow. It is only when one casts out evil loves that the transforming power of God can flow into the hearts and minds of those who are receptive. The more one leads a life of love and truth, the more closely that person is conjoined with God. And the more closely conjoined one is with God, the wiser that person can become because wisdom flows in from God to those who are receptive. This receptivity is made available by the emptying out of evil thoughts and actions and being in alignment with higher purposes.

Also, the more closely one is conjoined with God, the happier that person is. In any love—whether good or evil—there are delights or pleasures. The pleasure of affection for doing good grows into eternity; however, evil pleasures coming from love of self, not God, do not continue to bring joy. One can compare the pleasure of evil to the fun of frogs in a cold, dark swamp, while delights of love are like the joy of a butterfly in a warm, sunny flower garden. The happiness from loving and doing good is not always obvious in the natural world, but is often felt as peace of mind or ease. Once a person is in heaven, however, true happiness is felt in its fullness.

Another characteristic of people who are closely aligned with God is that they sense themselves to be freer and more their own person, not bound by unnecessary restrictions, but operating in freedom. The irony is that the more someone appears to be independent in thoughts and actions, the more closely that person recognizes the source from whence the love and wisdom originate. The more one recognizes God's interaction in one's life, the wiser, happier, and freer they become. This is the purpose of these spiritual laws, or Divine providence.

Spiritual Law Is Infinite and Eternal

It is important to understand the concepts of infinity and eternity in order to understand aspects of God or the Divine. Infinity and eternity are difficult for the natural, or finite, mind to grasp primarily because the natural mind operates under the limitations of time and space, while the spiritual does not. However, it is possible to understand the existence of these concepts, even if we cannot grasp their full nature. One way to think of infinity and eternity is to see that, according to angelic wisdom, the infinite is the Divine being of God and the eternal is the Divine expression of God and together they comprise the nature of God.

It may be difficult for people to understand this idea of infinity and eternity if they can think only from a natural perspective because it takes more interior or spiritual thinking to comprehend this idea. Just as it is hard to conceive of love or wisdom in terms of space and time, so is it difficult to think of the infinite or eternal in the same way. It requires a more spiritually rational mind to see the Divine in these concepts.

Another way of understanding the quality of the spiritual is to observe that a person can regard another only in terms of their own nature. In other words, people can only recognize the love or wisdom in another if they also have these qualities. If they do not, they will not be able to see them in others. So it is with God, who can be joined with people only to the level of their love and wisdom. Thus, if the basic nature of some people is evil, it is impossible for God to dwell within them.

The paradox is that this connection has to originate from God, from the infinite to the finite, and not the other way around. However, we can prepare the way and invite God into our lives by living a life of love and shunning those actions that are evil. Subsequently, the Divine can come in and be an influence and driving force, leading one through trials with strength and wisdom, and awakening the soul to joy.

We can witness evidence of infinity and eternity in the natural world in the endless variety of facial features, temperaments, and affections of people. We can also see among the many types of plants, animals, and humans that the drive to propagate is part of a never-ending endeavor to reproduce—from creation to eternity. We see the many ways in which people have sought wisdom and realize that we can never know everything. There will always be areas to explore and new knowledge to gain. The fact that these expressions of eternity and infinity exist within humans who continue to reproduce and continue to search for wisdom is evidence of the influence of God, who is infinity and eternity.

However, humans are finite and can have nothing of infinity

within them except as emanations of God. They can be seen merely as the vessels that receive this love and wisdom, also known as infinity and eternity. Even though it appears as that they act from these qualities out of their own natures, they are, in fact, vessels to be filled with God's love.

The purpose of these spiritual laws is the unification of Divine love and wisdom within each human being, which creates a heavenly state and leads one to heaven in the next world. Thus it can be said that the goal of Divine providence is to create a heaven from human beings, or angels from the human species, so that all can dwell in a state of Divine love and wisdom unto eternity.

On the other hand, in freedom one can pursue evil and false affections in this world, and therefore choose to live in a hellish state in the next world. When we become aware of what these spiritual laws are, we can more easily choose which path we want to follow. Ultimately, it is up to each human being, day by day, to make the decisions that determine which loves they follow, what choices they make. Having some awareness of how God governs the world and for what purpose might illuminate the way and make the journey easier and more joyful.

◊ Five Spiritual Laws

There are five basic spiritual laws by which Divine providence operates and the in-depth examination of each law will help explain its application to a person's life. Looking at each law is essential to recognize its influence. In fact, if spiritual laws are not known, it is easy for people mistakenly to take credit for the good things they have done, or to think that chance or bad luck is responsible for all tragedies. Still worse, when sad events occur, some people think that God intentionally causes this suffering. In order to progress spiritually, we need to learn these spiritual laws in order to lift a veil of mystery that has surrounded human understanding. These five spiritual laws are as follows:

1. *People are free to act according to their understanding of right and wrong.*

2. *When people turn away from evil in their external thoughts and actions, God can transform the internal or spiritual body.*

3. *People are responsible for their own spiritual transformation and are not dependent upon something or someone else to make them change.*

4. *We are led and taught by God although it appears we are doing everything ourselves.*

5. *Even though a person may not know how and when these spiritual laws operate, it is still possible to acknowledge their existence and influence.*

1. People are free to act according to their understanding of right and wrong.

Humans are born with two basic spiritual and mental capacities that give able individuals the capacity to choose. The first is the ability to understand, which is called *rationality*. The second is the ability to act on this understanding, called *freedom*, which can include actions such as speaking or writing or fulfilling an intention.

In general, freedom is connected to the loves and desires of one's life. Just as a river draws one along in its current, so does a person's love take them in the direction of its object. To begin to understand how we can choose which stream in which to flow, we need to see that different types of freedom reflect different types of loves. These freedoms are described as natural freedom, rational freedom, and spiritual freedom.

Natural freedom is part of our fallible human nature, our instinctual side, and concerns itself with self-love and a love of the world. These two loves are the root of all evil and following these desires exclusively results in the expression of evil in the world. When selfish loves are justified by reason— a misuse of rationality—a person might commit adultery, fraud, revenge, and any number of deeds from the influence of this negative state unless controlled by civil law. But because a person is in freedom from God and rationally justifies their actions, a person can act solely from this natural freedom.

Rational freedom is a step higher. It puts a significant value on reputation for the purpose of gain or honor in the world. Consequently, a person acting from rational freedom may appear more moral than someone acting from natural freedom. This person may know that adultery, blasphemy, and fraud are wrong, and thus avoid them for the external reason of reputation, not for the internal reason that they are wrong and acts against God. If rational behavior comes from a selfish, not spiritual source, then the good deeds a person does are not really good since they are performed solely for reputation and honor. In this kind of person, rational freedom represents a more interior form of natural freedom, but more external than spiritual.

Spiritual freedom comes when a person chooses not to do or say evil things because they are wrong, and then turns to God as the source of a higher love. It is this higher, more elevated love that gives a person full capacity of expression. Although it may not seem like freedom at the time, in looking back one can see that this path helps to control the desires of natural instincts and purifies rational justification so that one thinks, wills, and ultimately does good.

To understand these different levels of freedom, it is helpful to look to the various types of motivations and their correlating partners. The motivation behind natural love is knowledge; behind rational love, intelligence; behind heavenly love, wisdom. Animals have only the first level of motivation and thus are ruled by desires and knowledge. They have no ability to reason and to act in freedom according to reason. Humans, however, have the capacity to elevate their motives through their intellect and they also have the ability to choose to do this. For people who have no desire to understand anything other than the physical world and do not want to elevate themselves, they will remain in knowledge only. The doors to intelligence and wisdom will be closed. Thus, although they still retain the faculties of reason and freedom, they operate in the world more as animals, driven only by their instinctual natures.

Paradoxically, when we understand that although people are guided throughout their lives by God—whether they realize it or not—it appears to them as though all of their thoughts and actions originate from themselves. They willingly take credit and feel good about themselves for the good deeds they do and kind words they say. It is a necessary component of rationality and freedom that people feel this way because, without this quality, people would not look to their own reasoning, choose to be more loving, and turn to God for help. They would not be propelled forward to continue doing good if they did not think they were responsible.

As part of this process, when a person begins to refrain from doing evil, their rationality and freedom increase and they begin to recognize the source of all power, which is God. Thus, we can appreciate the paradox that people think they are responsible for all their good deeds until they reach a state of consciousness where they can recognize the true source. In the early stages of development, however, this information would be very difficult to understand and might actually limit a person's progress.

Whatever a person does based on reason and freedom becomes part of that person's character permanently. Even if, for example, people led lives of depravity and evil, then changed their ways and called upon God to elevate their inclinations and deeds, those earlier acts would still be part of their character. The focus of their current lives would be very different since they would not be following evil inclinations, but these evil deeds would remain at the periphery of their being. An exception to this is if one thinks about doing something evil, but chooses not to do it. This evil does not become part of that person's essential character since a person decided not to commit the act. However, if they want to commit evil, but are kept in check by fear or external means, this is the same as if they had actually done it and it will remain part of their character. Thus is the spiritual meaning of the passage in Matthew 15: 11-20 where Jesus deals with criticism from the elders that he was not following tradition because he did not insist that his followers wash their hands before eating:

> It is not what goes into the mouth that defiles a person, but it is what comes out of the mouth that defiles. . . . Do you not see that whatever goes into the mouth enters the stomach and goes out the sewer? But what comes out of the mouth proceeds from the heart, and this is what defiles. For out of the heart come evil intentions, murder, adultery, fornication, theft, false witness, slander. These are what defile a person.

It is through freedom and reason that one can be reformed and able to lead a good life. This is called *spiritual transformation*—the shift from a natural or physical existence where love of the self and the world is at the center to a spiritual focus where love of God and others is the central motivating force in one's life. To understand this process, it helps to examine the stages that one has to pass through. The first is a natural state, based on human heredity and natural freedom, where the only love is oneself and a desire to dominate others and possess wealth. People in this stage remain in a hellish internal state of mind and do not allow themselves to be transformed into a higher form of love.

The second stage, repentance and reformation, occurs when one starts to think about the joy of heaven. This thought usually begins from a perspective of self-interest and is based on the desire for heavenly delights that one anticipates. Many believe that the way to heaven consists of doing such things as praying, serving the poor, attending religious services, making donations, and giving to the needy. This concept is based on a simplistic understanding of religion, where one does good deeds for the sole reason of getting to heaven. Although these deeds are important, real transformation begins when people begin to understand that evil deeds are, in fact, acts against God. They also recognize that evil or sin does exist, and then they go through a period of reflection and self-examination.

The next step is regeneration, the state of spiritual transformation, which follows the stage of reformation. At this point, the order of one's life changes. A person will choose not to do evil because of love of God and, when tempted, will call upon God's help to overcome these inclinations. This is the process of becoming a spiritual person. And even though people may have committed evil acts earlier in their lives, the good that now governs them is a mitigating factor and thus they are not condemned.

The faculties of rationality and freedom are at the heart of these processes and allow a person to elevate his or her consciousness. Realizing that God is the source of all good and truth is a necessary step in spiritual development. Another component is living a life according to the principles based on this belief, such as following the Golden Rule and the Ten Commandments or the tenets of one's faith.

Every connection between people or between a person and God implies reciprocity, which, in this case, involves loving the neighbor as oneself and loving God above all. Loving all people is a necessary component of loving God and produces a covenant that is a connection with God. One who does not love others is incapable of loving God.

These two qualities of freedom and rationality are held sacred and kept intact throughout people's lives, whether they have evil or good intentions. People are given the ability to understand what they are willing to grasp and, through their freedom, they can connect with God's will, begin to reform their lives, and live a heavenly existence.

It is, therefore, the goal of God's spiritual laws that people act in freedom according to their understanding. Even if people act from natural freedom and choose a selfish existence, God guards these qualities of freedom and reason to give them the capacity for changing. The infernal freedom of evil can be replaced with heavenly freedom if one wills it. God is always there to continually lead one away from evil words and deeds.

There are exceptions where some people are not able to reform themselves, including those who are unable to develop full rational abilities or whose minds have become too damaged to function properly. Nor can children have access to full rational abilities until their minds mature. Others who will have difficulty include those who adamantly deny the existence of God or any higher power, and those who attribute all to natural law, in opposition to the existence of God. It is the goal of spiritual law to bring a person to a state of genuine freedom and rationality, a state in which one shuns evils as sins and acknowledges the source of all love and wisdom from our Creator. This begins the process of transformation of a person from a natural to a spiritual being.

2. It is only when people turn away from evil in their external thoughts and actions that God can transform the internal or spiritual body.

Another way of stating this spiritual law is that God cannot enter a person until that person shuns evil. This statement represents a microcosm of both heaven and hell, where good is heaven and evil is hell. It is impossible for good and evil to coexist in the same space. Therefore, hell must be removed for heaven to enter.

Many people do not acknowledge the presence of evil and therefore do not think about their evil inclinations. If they do not examine their own actions and choose to cease pursuing negative delights, then evil will control them. Just as a person in the dark cannot see, a person who does not think about such things cannot see good or evil. Perhaps they dismiss this thinking as unimportant because they believe that, in the end, all will be forgiven because of their faith. In the spiritual world, however, it is a person's life that determines their faith and not the other way around. Therefore, it is necessary for a person to recognize the evil within themselves and cease pursuing these evil thoughts and actions so that God may bring that person to a heavenly state.

Each person has two levels of thought or self: internal and external. The external body or person generally acts according to the internal spirit. However, everyone knows that one can think or intend something internally, but conduct oneself differently on the outside by overriding these thoughts. We know this because when we listen to others, we sometimes try to evaluate the sincerity of their words and try to determine the speaker's intention and whether that person is to be believed. Thus we can recognize the hypocrites and those who flatter for their own sake. These people think one thing on the inside and express a contrary action on the outside.

A person's internal thought comes from their affections or loves; the external comes from memory or serves as a means to an end. From childhood until adolescence, the external loves help to form the internal ones; all of the nurturing a person receives from parents and teachers helps to shape their affections. After that, a person's real life becomes their internal affections and perceptions; the external thought is the means for this internal love.

Another way of understanding this is seeing it as source, cause, and effect. One's life's loves are the source, its affections and perceptions the cause, and the delights and thoughts of this affection is the effect. These loves can be either heavenly or hellish, as compared to either a fruit-bearing tree or a spider and its web. Heavenly love is like the tree, whose leaves are affections for good and the fruits are the delight. Hellish loves are like the spider who weaves a web of cunning and deception in order to trap the delights of lust, which are then consumed by the spider.

In general, the character of the external thought is similar to that of the internal, although sometimes disguised.

At times it seems as though a person's external expression is different from their internal loves. This comes about by means of an internal censor that keeps internal lusts under control in the outward expression, usually because of legal restrictions or reputation. Examples of this include the hypocrite who says one thing while believing something else and insincere priests who preach a love of God and of others while not actually believing. Judges who take bribes, but speak of justice, and businessmen who are at heart crooked, but present themselves as honest, are other examples. When people who are ruled by heavenly loves, however, their internal censors watch out only that their expressions be as truthful and good as their motivations.

For spiritual transformation on the internal level, it is an essential first step that external evil words and deeds be eliminated.

The external negativity of these actions creates a delight that feeds the internal desire, thus making transformation impossible. Just as a person who loves to steal or lie will continue until caught, so evil grows if not placed under restraints. The evil becomes like a fire raging out of control or gangrene that eats away at one's body.

By their own accord through self-reflection and repentance, people can stop committing evil. There are sacred customs, such as before Holy Communion or during Rosh Hashannah, where one examines one's life, identifies sins, and repents by rejecting them. This process is useful for these times and also can be practiced during individual reflection anytime. This is the way God can transform a person. It is only by individual reflection and repentance that this transformation can happen, along with the realization that one must turn away from sins for one reason only—that they are against loving God.

Once a person chooses to reject evil in their life, it is like a door has opened to allow God to enter. At this point, God can not only purify people of the delights that come from negative external pursuits, but God can also cleanse their lust or desire for evil internally. This is the meaning in the book of Revelation 3:19-20:

> Be earnest, therefore, and repent. Listen! I am standing at the door, knocking; if you hear my voice and open the door, I will come in to you and eat with you, and you with me.

This process is the way that God can purify a person. Good acts, going to church, and reading the Bible are all valuable things to do, but the only way for real transformation is to invite God in by self-examination, cessation of evil, and repentance. It is the goal of spiritual law, or Divine providence, that God be joined to all people in accordance with their own freedom and ability to reason.

This process that God uses to transform a person works simultaneously on the external and internal aspects of a person. Although a person may not know most of the elements of their inner thoughts, they can cease saying and doing evil things and look to God in order to transform themselves into spiritual beings. The opportunity for God to come into a person's life is made possible by this awareness of the importance of doing good and ceasing to choose evil.

The reward of living a new life, of choosing to focus one's energies on expressing good and truth, is eternal life. This is what is discussed in Matthew 7:15-20:

> Beware of false prophets, who come to you in sheep's
> clothing but inwardly are ravenous wolves. You will know
> them by their fruits. Are grapes gathered from thorns, or
> figs from thistles? In the same way, every good tree bears

good fruit, but the bad trees bear bad fruit. A good tree cannot bear bad fruit, nor can a bad tree bear good fruit. Every tree that does not bear good fruit is cut down and thrown into the fire. Thus you will know them by their fruits.

3. It is up to all people to work on their own spiritual transformation and not depend on something or someone else to make them change.

According to spiritual law, the form of people's lives is based on the choices they make, in freedom according to their understanding. To be compelled by external forces would run counter to the two previous spiritual laws because external force conflict with freedom as well as individual choice. A person cannot be forced to think or love or believe what is not true to that person. Even if one is forced to speak in favor of something that is not believed, their internal beliefs are not touched. Nothing external can create change for the internal self.

It helps to examine what events possibly might compel a person to change. One case to consider is whether one can change belief systems through miracles. This would be problematic because basing your faith on external factors, such as miracles, does not represent a true change of heart and mind, which develops from inner understanding and rational thought.

God transforms from the internal through the external person. If a person were to change based on external occurrences, it would close the door to influence from God since it would be only an external transformation without the corresponding internal one. It would be the same if one accepted a belief system without careful examination and understanding of its implications. People of faith who hear of or witness miracles see them as confirmation of their faith, not justification of it. Their faith comes from an understanding of sacred scripture, living a life of goodness and truth, and experiencing Divine presence.

If unbelievers witness miracles, any transformation would be short lived, since it would be external and would not change their internal loves.

Visions, too, cannot be the basis for true reformation. Heavenly visions are from a spiritual source and one must be in a spiritual state to witness them, but there are also visions that can come from hellish states and mislead. Communication with the dead or other-worldly encounters cannot transform a person either. Real transformation comes from self-examination and repentance and spiritual guidance from God's teachings.

Nor can one effectively use threats or punishment to force others to change their internal loves. In fact, the opposite often happens when one tries to compel another to change. Their ideas are pushed away because it is the internal self that compels the external, and not the other way around. From this it can be seen that it is not useful to force anyone to worship if they do not wish to do so. Forced worship closes the internal self off from the external and can block in evils that smolder, as a fire smolders under the ash until it bursts into flame. Voluntary worship in contrast is like a fire built in the open that burns quickly and completely. Elective worship is joyful and alive, while forced religion is dull and lifeless.

People can experience spiritual transformation only if they are in a state of freedom and have rational capabilities. However, there are some physical and mental states in which this is not possible, including a state of fear, physical or mental illness, ignorance, or blocked intellect. Each of these will be discussed.

1. *Fear:* Fear is a part of external thought that blocks internal transformation. If one is totally consumed with fears about their human condition, reputation, physical survival, and wealth, they are not open to God's influence. If one is fearful of loss of heaven, however, this does not block the influence from God because this is a spiritual concern and can be addressed with reason and understanding.

2. *Physical and mental illness*: If one's mind or body is not

sound, that person cannot be rational and free. Certain mental states, such as depression, mental distress, and grief block a person from thinking clearly as do certain physical states. One example is deathbed transformations, which are most likely expressions of words rather than a true transformation of the spirit. However, if a person has already begun the reformation process before illness, this is often an effective time to turn one's mind to God.

3. *Ignorance:* People raised in a state of ignorance cannot have the understanding necessary for transformation.

4. *Blocked intellect:* This state occurs when one's understanding has been blocked by false teaching, which precludes truth. Other states, such as lust, can also make a person unaware of truth and of transformation of the spirit.

As we have discussed earlier, the internal and external minds are distinct and can operate independently from each other. For some people, external expression is very different from internal thought. In others, the internal thought and external action are connected so that they do what they think and believe. This is usually true of honest people, while the disconnected state between internal and external reflects that of a dishonest person.

Thus it is possible for the internal and external to be in opposition at times. Internally, if one knows what is true and good, but feels drawn to commit acts that are not, a battle can ensue. This is called a *temptation*. When the internal self compels the external to follow what is good, rather than succumb to the temptation, it opens the way for God to flow in.

It is within the realm of freedom and rationality for the internal to put pressure on the external to desist from doing evil. Resisting temptation opens the door to greater freedom and keeps a person from the hellish state of being controlled by human nature.

The process of overcoming temptation works this way because the external self is reformed from the internal, not the other way around. The influence flows from the spiritual to the natural, not the reverse. This is what is meant in Matthew 23: 25-26:

> Woe to you, scribes and Pharisees, hypocrites! For you clean the outside of the cup and of the plate, but inside they are full of greed and self-indulgence. You blind Pharisee! First clean the inside of the cup so that the outside also may become clean.

There are preliminary stages that a person goes through in the process of spiritual transformation. First, after self-examination, a person progresses to a purification process that involves looking at one's external actions as well as internal longings. The person realizes that evil comes from hellish sources and good from heaven. The person can then choose to look to heaven.

The second comes when that person chooses to refrain from doing evil. The external is transformed by the inner understanding, but this process of reformation, repentance, and transformation is not complete until the external follows the internal motivation to do good.

4. We are led and taught by God although it appears that we are doing everything ourselves.

There is a difference between the appearance and reality of what we do and say. For example, a person may take credit for the learning and knowledge they have acquired, although the reality is that God is behind this process. Those who see only the manifestation of a situation, but not the reality, are in a state of natural rationality. But those who see the appearance and also the reality that God is the source are in a state of spiritual rationality. Another way of looking at the difference between these two ways of perception is thinking of the first as being a garden in winter—with light and cold—and the second as a garden in the spring—with light and warmth.

This fourth spiritual law explains that we are led and taught by God although it appears that we are doing everything ourselves. This is a very difficult concept to grasp, and one that might not be fully understandable in this world. However, it is possible to look at this idea rationally. First of all, for all life to exist there must be a source of all life, which could be called Divine essence, or Divine love and wisdom. Second, since we have the ability to think and to love, these capacities must originate from the original emanation of love and wisdom, which is from God. And because a person's life follows from this will and intellect, which come from God, it points to where all of our strength, love, and wisdom come. The understanding that God is absolute good and truth is fundamental to recognizing our love and wisdom as derivative and dependent upon the original source.

Several passages in the Bible convey this concept, such as in the Gospel of John:

> No one can receive anything except what has been given
> from heaven. (3:27)

I am the resurrection and the life. Those who believe in me, even though they die, will live, and everyone who lives and believes in me will never die. (11:25)

I am the way, the truth, and the life. (14:6)

This influence from God flows into the good and evil people alike. What differs is the form that receives it, not the source. Thus human beings reflect a variety of forms and manifestations of God's love and wisdom. Just as natural heat and light flow into a garden and produce a variety of plant forms, so do spiritual warmth and light—love and wisdom—flow into the minds of people who in turn produce diverse results. Where it comes from, however, is the same for all.

All people, whether angels or mortals, are joined with God in direct proportion to their reception of love and wisdom. Each person has a unique place and role to serve, whether on earth or in heaven, which often requires much searching. Those who stay open to the inflow of love from God will find their eternal home; those that do not will separate themselves from this source.

A person is led by spiritual influence, which is love from God, and is taught by enlightenment, which is wisdom from God. Just as blood flows into the heart, so does the love of God flow into a person's motivations. Likewise, the internal sight of a person, which is called *intellect,* is enhanced by spiritual light. Different from the natural version, this spiritual light is divine in origin. The awakening of a person who is taught by God through this spiritual light allows them to perceive truth internally. There is also an exterior enlightenment from God that draws from the interior insights and allows one to consider both sides of an issue and then, with clarity, dismiss the incorrect interpretation.

Another type of interior and exterior influence is one that comes from a person, not from God, and this is very different.

People in this state draw from their personal knowledge and see things in relation to their own selfish desires. They are not able to recognize truth, but only use information and memory to justify what they want. Thus, in order to be able to recognize truth and be taught by it, one needs to look to guidance from God.

Therefore, we need to discover how God teaches us. There are sacred writings that can be used for inspiration and guidance, such as the *Bhagavad Gita*, Buddhist texts, and ones from enlightened mystics. We also can turn to the word of God, the Bible, that is considered by many to be of divine origin. These holy writings are ways that God conveys wisdom into human minds; thus to read the Bible and other sacred books is to be taught by and be in communication with God.

This is seen in the book of John:

In the beginning was the Word and the Word was with God, and the Word was God. (1:1)

Later, it is said:

It is the spirit that gives life; the flesh is useless. The
words I have spoken to you are spirit and life. (6:63)

In addition to receiving guidance by reading sacred writings,
a person can be taught by wise people in their lives, such as
teachers, parents, and preachers. In this way, it is possible for all
to become spiritual beings by following the tenets of their own
religions, which would include loving God and likewise loving
other people. Although we can learn many truths by reading the
word of God, the full extent of the meaning may not be obvious
until these works are read from a heavenly perspective in the next
world.

In all appearance, it seems that people think and act from
their own intelligence, which is a stage necessary in order to
function and learn to become receptive to guidance from God.

Later, as a person is more closely connected to spiritual influence, it is obvious that the source of all love and wisdom is God. Thus we have the appearance that we do everything ourselves, while the reality reveals something quite different as we advance along the path of greater understanding.

5. Even though a person may not know how and when these spiritual laws operate, it is still possible to acknowledge their existence and influence.

It is easy to see how someone might view the successes of evil people and conclude that Divine providence does not exist. They might decide that cunning and deceit are the secret to success, instead of truth and goodness. This is how the natural mind works—attributing nothing to God, only to the natural world. However, from a spiritual point of view one can recognize the workings of Divine providence without being aware of all the steps of its operation; otherwise it would be almost impossible not to interfere and influence the results by one's own preferences and desires.

According to the first spiritual law, a person acts in freedom according to their understanding and everything a person does appears to come from that person alone. If people were able to perceive God's influence in their lives, they would not feel free to choose their own actions. A perception of these laws in operation, of God's leading people to good, would upset the equilibrium between good and evil and could interfere with a person's salvation. Likewise, if one were able to predict the future, it would be almost impossible not to intrude in some way. We would lose the human experience of wanting and hoping for something if we knew what was going to happen. Therefore, people can have the confidence of knowing that God is guiding their lives, but live without direct knowledge so that they do not interfere with the workings.

We are all aware of the fact that there are inner and outer workings of the body. The skin covers the veins, organs, and other parts of the body that make it function. We can direct the way our outer body operates, but for the most part do not direct the functions of our inner body. It is the same with Divine providence. We can direct our outer choices in what kind of life we lead, but if we were aware of all of the inner spiritual influences, we most likely would interfere and disrupt the process.

Another reason that we are shielded from full knowledge of the workings of spiritual law is the risk that if we were to clearly see its workings, we might take personal credit for this knowledge and consider ourselves to be divine, or in control of all elements of our lives. In this situation, we would deny any influence from God, thus denying the existence of God. A person's natural inclinations turn toward selfish ends; it is Divine providence that directs one toward overcoming these natural desires and transforming them to more spiritual loves. However, if people were aware of this influence as it happened, it would push them further away from spiritual direction and more toward natural ends.

Therefore, Divine providence is not apparent, but is more like a stream drawing someone along toward the good. Its tendency is to humble the proud and exalt the humble in an atmosphere of freedom. If we were to be aware, our human tendency would be to interfere, misinterpret, or rebel against its influence.

Those of a natural mind, who might want to see the future in advance, have not developed the ability to recognize the unfoldment of spiritual law in their lives by reflecting on past events. Instead, they attribute all incidents to natural cause since they can see things only from a natural perspective. People who have become spiritual can recognize things as they really are: natural things are seen naturally; spiritual matters are recognized as spiritual. A natural person is like a near-sighted person in a garden filled with fruit. This person cannot recognize the bounty that surrounds them and would comment that they only saw green trees, not recognizing the fruit there as well. Or they are like a person who visits a beautiful cathedral and hears an uplifting sermon and only reports hearing talking in a building.

As we develop our spiritual natures, either in this world or the next, we are aware of the beautiful unfolding of spiritual law. This is clear looking back, rather than forward, and eventually we will recognize the action of God in our lives in retrospect, from a spiritual perspective.

Characteristics of Spiritual Law

To be able to put these spiritual laws into practice, it is helpful to understand their application and specific characteristics. For example, it would be valuable to consider how we receive the wisdom to transform ourselves. Religious traditions teach us that it comes from God, while the world teaches that it comes from the knowledge of an individual. To understand the connection between these ideas, it would help to explore some of the characteristics of how this wisdom is acquired.

The key force behind one's thoughts is the ruling motivation or affections of a person. The loves of one's life are what give pleasure and delight; the thoughts find satisfaction in their consideration. What forms a person's life is the combination of the two—affections and thoughts—and the delight and satisfaction they produce. In the body they are natural; in the mind, spiritual. This combination produces an atmosphere that represents the unique character of that person.

From one's natural character comes the hereditary soul, which is the source of love of self and the world. This love of self wants attention for itself and regards others as inferior. Its companion is the intellect, which manifests as conceit or a sense of pride that promotes the belief that all wisdom comes from within that individual. When one chooses this path, one lives in a hellish state.

However, if people can set aside love for the self and allow themselves to express love for the neighbor, they are in a heavenly state. This allows the love from God to flow into their affections and allows them to be led by Divine providence. It appears as though an individual's wisdom is responsible for making all choices, but it is actually the ceasing to do evil and doing good that invite God to come into one's life and provide heavenly influence. If this interaction were not so well disguised, one's natural character would block God's influence. God's interaction through Divine providence can be compared to a person who leads a friend to safety away from an enemy, unbeknownst to them, and who later learns and informs the friend of the danger they were in. Thus God leads us, while always allowing us the freedom to follow.

Temporary and Eternal Aspects of Spiritual Law

Another characteristic of spiritual law is that it focuses on eternal matters, not temporary ones except as they coexist with eternal ones. One example of worldly, temporary goals is the love of money and position, which comes from a desire to dominate others and be considered superior to them. However, it is possible to possess a love of being in a powerful position and having wealth in order to do good for others. This represents a heavenly state internally even though externally it may appear similar to the love of money and power for worldly reasons.

Sometimes it seems as though riches and honors are blessings and other times they are curses. The difference is whether one loves these things for selfish reasons or whether they love them for the good that can be created for others. Thus, riches and power can lead evil people astray when they arouse the love of self; in other people these gifts can be put to good use. When we look carefully, we see that one is temporary and fleeting because it considers only the material things of the world for one's self interest; the other is eternal and spiritual because it focuses on doing good for others.

These two motivations is considered in the Gospel of Matthew 6:19-21:

> Do not store up for yourselves treasures on earth, where moth and rust consume and where thieves break in and steal; but store up for yourselves treasures in heaven, where neither moth nor rust consumes and where thieves do not break in and steal. For where your treasure is, there your heart will be also.

Temporary things depend upon space and time, or what has a limit or end. However, what relates to God is eternal, never ending. In fact, nothing eternal can come from a temporary being unless it is the eternal working through the finite, which comes as a result of an alignment of temporary and eternal things through the workings of spiritual law.

How God Protects People

Since all spiritual laws are designed to lead people to heaven and salvation it would seem that God, in omnipotence, could save everyone simply by willing it so. However, this would rob us of our freedom and run counter to the spiritual law discussed earlier about people having the freedom to choose according to reason.

God protects people from making grave mistakes by opening up truths of faith and charity to the degree that a person is able to maintain them throughout a lifetime without misusing them. Although some people can understand wisdom and heavenly love naturally, they may not have transformed internally. People can rationally comprehend goodness and act accordingly, but it may not come from their core character. These are hypocrites who act on the outside a certain way, but inside have evil or selfish motives. However, covering up one's true state is not possible in the next world. A symbol of this state is represented in the story of the man who appears at the wedding feast without a proper garment in Matthew 22:11-13:

> But when the king came in to see the guests, he noticed a man there who was not wearing a wedding robe, and he said to him, 'Friend, how did you get in here without a wedding robe?' And he was speechless. Then the king said to the attendants, 'Bind him hand and foot and throw him into the outer darkness where there will be weeping and gnashing of teeth.' For many are called, but few are chosen.

One leaves the outer garments behind when one enters the spiritual world and one's inner qualities become transparent to all those around.

However, there is a condition that is much more damaging than hypocrisy. It is very dangerous to one's spiritual development to be aware of and accept spiritual truths and then turn away and act contrary to these truths. It would have been better if they had not been acknowledged at all. Understanding this spiritual state comes from a very esoteric principle, which needs to be explained. Acknowledging God, and the good and truth that comes from that acknowledgment, opens up one's interior to heavenly influence. A subsequent denial of this will cause good and evil to be mixed in one's internal nature, which creates a very unhealthy situation. This is a state of extreme depravity, where one cannot distinguish between good and evil because they are so mixed. Profaners, religious leaders who misuse their power and teachers who knowingly lead the young astray fall into this category.

There are many ways in which a person is protected from this state of depravity. For example, a person who is ignorant cannot misuse sacred wisdom from God in pursuit of their own selfish motives because they have not been taught the truth. Also free from this state are children and young people who learn truths from childhood and then turn away from them because part of the natural intellectual development of a person is to choose their faith for themselves. Likewise, a person who lives a selfish life and then turns to living a life based on wisdom from God does not mix good and evil in their internal nature. The original evil is kept separate from the good that comes from choosing a life based on spiritual principles, which includes love of God and love of the neighbor.

Only those who acknowledge the sacredness of God, the holiness of the Bible, and the importance of church, and still condemn these things can desecrate them. People who deny God or spiritual matters cannot defame what they do not recognize. The importance of this principle is the focus of the second commandment, which states that you should not take the name of God in vain, and in the Lord's Prayer, which states, "Hallowed be Thy name."

Sometimes these incidents of desecration slip into our speech through laziness or lack of awareness. This happens every time we use the name of God in anger or as a joke. The seriousness of a person's offense is in relation to how sacred the Scriptures or holy teaching are to that person. In any case, it indicates contempt for God in some degree and therefore warrants attention and self-examination. Another example of this state is acknowledging the truth of spiritual laws but living in a way that does not support this acknowledgment.

A more serious example is using the literal sense of the Bible to defend or support evil or falsity, which is a misuse of the sacred for selfish purposes. Other examples include hypocrites who speak piously while harboring evil motives or those who take on Divine attributes for themselves. The worst case, mentioned earlier, are those who affirm spiritual truths and then proceed to deny them because good and evil are mixed within these people. This is what is meant by those who are lukewarm in the following passage from the book of Revelation 3:15-16:

> I know your works; you are neither cold nor hot. I wish that you were either cold or hot. So, because you are lukewarm, and neither cold nor hot, I am about to spit you out of my mouth.

God introduces elements of good and truth into a person's inner thought to the degree that evil and falsity have been removed. This is done as a person opens up more and more to spiritual influence, as described in the following passage from the book of Revelation 3:20:

Listen, I am standing at the door, knocking; if you hear my
voice and open the door, I will come in to you and eat with
you, and you with me.

The way a person invites God in is by resisting evil and embrac-
ing good.

Good from God can come in only to the degree that the evil
exits. This process can be described as rooms in a house, where
the good is introduced from the outside into the most interior
spaces to the extent that one is able to use it appropriately. A
different situation governs the intellect, where wisdom or truth
is stored. As we learn and grow, we need to be taught truths that
will be available if we choose to reorder our lives to live an unselfish rather than a selfish life. We store these truths in memory
where we can access them when and if we long for the spiritual
wisdom contained within. In this way truth and falsity do not
mix, but are kept separate. Thus, God protects us from our own

weaknesses of possibly misusing sacred information by introducing it only when we are able to recognize its holiness and use it in a responsible way.

Spiritual Laws and the Laws of Permission

It is often difficult to understand how God can allow evil events and criminal people to exist, but these are permitted under the operation of spiritual law. The key point to understand is that God provides spiritual law for the salvation of the world, but evil is also allowed. It is not willed by God, but is permitted to safeguard our freedom.

When we look at examples of evil throughout the Bible, we might wonder why God did not intervene to stop these acts. Consider the time that the children of Israel were allowed to worship the golden calf while Moses was on Mount Sinai. We can begin to understand how this was permitted in order to save them. The people still carried within them the internal love of idols that had been taught to them in Egypt. This false teaching needed to be expressed outwardly through idols so that they could be taught the truth and punished for this misunderstanding. These and other stories can be explained in light of Divine providence when one sees that by permitting evil, God allows one to learn about good.

It is easy to see how someone can doubt the idea of spiritual law when they see evil people prospering at the expense of good people. Likewise, one can see the evidence of despicable people rising to positions of importance while well-meaning people are poor and powerless.

People look at war and do not understand how a loving God could permit this. On the other hand, how could that not be permitted if people are allowed to choose freely? Perhaps one of the only good results that can come of evil and destructive acts is the recognition of the fact that there are evil forces, which will have increasing influence if people do not pay attention. If these destructive events do occur, people can see what horrors may happen if there is not an awareness of consciously doing good, loving others, and loving God. Evil thrives in an atmosphere of complacency and ignorance. Perhaps one of the reasons evil is permitted is so that people can see it in form, not just theory, and thereby acknowledge its presence and be able to resist it.

All of the events of the world, called *luck* by some, come either from the influence of heaven, called Divine providence, or from the pull of evil, which God permits. We can trace evidence of both of these influences in the outcome of large events as well as in the small details of our lives.

One can look at the circumstances of war and realize it is not always the good leaders who win. Often people driven by selfish intentions perform better in war because they are compelled by a desire for dominance and recognition, while good people are motivated by justice and desire to protect others. In the case of conflict, one can in good faith protect one's country and fellow citizens from invasion by an enemy, but not invade another country for dominance.

The existence of different religions with seemingly conflicting beliefs raises a question about why God would allow such varied expressions of faith. Since the purpose of spiritual law is to lead people to heaven, one might wonder if there is only one true path or belief system. The fact is that all who honor the tenets of their faith have the capacity for salvation. Following a religious tradition would include: accepting guidelines for living in teachings such as the Ten Commandments, loving God, and serving the neighbor. In fact, the knowledge of God exists worldwide, in many forms and interpretations, and heaven is open to all who have faith in God and also do acts of charity for the neighbor.

No one is taught directly from heaven, but indirectly from reading the wisdom contained within the Bible and other holy texts. This is not the first step, however. The first step to leading a spiritual life is to refrain from doing evil, not just by hoping that faith carries one through all circumstances, but instead taking an active role in avoiding evil and doing good. All those who believe in a life in the next world, a life in heaven, will realize that there is a higher law than natural law that governs our actions. This is the spiritual law of Divine providence.

The Permission of Evil

People are born into a state of hereditary evil, which means that their primary motivation is that of self-interest. All enter this state at birth. However, the way to evolve from being motivated by self-interest to unselfish love is through self-examination. Many people ignore this step, delude themselves about their motives, and do not claim responsibility for their thoughts and actions. These are people who might confess their sins, not from a position of real inquiry, but only as a sense of obligation. Others might think this step of self-inquiry is unnecessary because they have faith, and do not see the need to act from a sense of charity. Some are so involved with the world that they ignore the consequences of their actions, or do not care to see that what they are doing is wrong. Unless one examines one's life and decides to change, it is impossible to remove these selfish intentions. This process takes time and cannot happen instantaneously as some people might think, or as those who preach instant salvation may say.

Therefore, evil is permitted for the ultimate goal of saving people from their own inherent love of self and of doing evil.

During self-reflection and self-examination, people can recognize the intention behind their actions and perhaps discover selfish motives. From societal and religious teachings they learn how to behave in a civil, moral, and spiritual manner and how to control evil impulses. They are able, with their reason and the help of God, to overcome these hereditary impulses and lead a life based on good intentions. Without the power of freedom and rationality, however, they would not be able to recognize evil and choose wisely. Evil is permitted so one can exercise this freedom to choose.

Spiritual Law Operates in Evil as Well as Good People

The nature of spiritual law is that it holds true for all people, no matter what their ultimate goals or intentions may be. This is described in Matthew 5:44-45:

Love your enemies and pray for those who persecute you, so that you may be children of your Father in heaven; for he makes his sun rise on the evil and on the good, and sends rain on the righteous and on the unrighteous.

With the influence of Divine providence, reflection, and self-examination, people can recognize truth and develop an affection for it if they choose to do so. Also allowed is the permission of evil, co-existing with the goodness in the world, since the experience of witnessing or expressing evil can be conducive to the ultimate goal of salvation. By recognizing these influences and choosing which to follow, a person can cease living a selfish life and turn toward loving what is good. This is the purpose of the permission of evil.

Every Person Has the Capacity to be Reformed

Every person born is intended to go to heaven and none is pre-destined for hell. People are born with the capacity to understand truth and to do good, and it is from these attributes one follows civil and moral laws and thus becomes a vessel for spiritual life. The process of living an honest, law-abiding life prepares one to become a spiritual person. In addition, once civic laws are fol-lowed and then expressed on a higher level, they become spiritual as well. For example, to treat a person in an honest, non-violent way is a reflection of civil and moral law; when one does so because of love of the neighbor, not just from fear of breaking the law, it becomes a spiritual principle as well. We are all here on earth so that we can prepare to go to heaven. If we choose not to, we are responsible—not fate, destiny, or bad luck.

The way we prepare for heaven is by acknowledging God's

existence, which produces a connection with God, while the denial of God creates a separation. The connection with God is strengthened by living a life according one's faith, and by putting this acknowledgment of God into action. Preparing for heaven also involves turning away from doing evil deeds because they go against the love of God.

One aspect of loving our neighbors is the recognition that God has provided religions for all and that these faiths have within them the necessary components to enable people to get to heaven. It would be difficult, almost inconceivable, to think that a person could be denied the right to heaven by our Creator because of their place of birth or religious background. In fact, all those that acknowledge God and fill their lives with love and truth are granted salvation.

God Cannot Act in Opposition to Spiritual Law

The expression of God is Divine love and Divine wisdom whose means of operation are through spiritual laws or Divine providence. The purpose of these laws is to direct people to heaven by means of following this divine order, which leads to salvation. Thus, it would be impossible for God to act against these spiritual laws because that would mean acting against divine intention.

This process of spiritual development begins at birth and continues throughout a person's life. Based on the direction of our thoughts and actions in this world, we are drawn to our innate loves in the other world and associate with people of similar affections. Meanwhile, God's love flows out toward all, with the hope of leading evil people away from greater evil and directing loving people to greater good. This operation of Divine providence continues throughout eternity and is done from a state of pure love and mercy.

 # Conclusion

This is the essence of Swedenborg's *Divine Providence*, or my understanding of his complete text in a shortened and restated version. I prepared an earlier example of this current work for my master's thesis in religious studies with the goal of learning how to communicate the deep, rich spiritual insights contained within Swedenborg's works with others. I was concerned that people would not find the time to wade through exhaustive texts for the incredible spiritual jewels within.

To get a clearer understanding of Swedenborg's publishing process and how he gained these insights, I have also included a chapter on his "call to publish" that follows this conclusion. It will help the reader understand the mission Swedenborg felt compelled to fulfill by both receiving revelation about the spiritual worlds and also writing about his findings. His insights fill over thirty volumes, so this overview of *Divine Providence* covers only a small part of his opus.

I found the book *Divine Providence* invaluable in its clarity about spiritual transformation through the workings of Divine providence. Swedenborg's poignant explanations can remove misunderstandings about this process and can clarify much for the serious spiritual seeker. He writes with the precision of a scientist about spiritual matters and outlines step-by-step how transformation works, while also offering guidance about how to lead the most loving and joyful life you might imagine.

If these ideas interest you, there are suggestions for further reading at the end of this book. Swedenborg was a scientist, theologian, philosopher, and mystic, so there are many aspects of his writings that may resonate with people of varying backgrounds, particularly those on a spiritual path since it is available to all religions and benevolent belief systems. He tells us how Divine love and wisdom flow into humans and how we can access this inexhaustible energy. Swedenborg tells us how the universe operates according to spiritual laws, much as we understand the physical laws that govern our material existence. Knowledge of these spiritual laws gives us awareness of choice, an explanation of evil, and steps for spiritual transformation.

It is from my love of this work and its influence on my life that I wish to share these insights with others. When we go with the current of Divine providence, rather than fighting against it, life becomes more peaceful and loving. Now that we have this knowledge of how the spiritual world interacts with the natural, we can apply these insights as we journey along the stream of providence, following our heart's greatest love.

Swedenborg's "Call to Publish"

For twenty-seven years, from 1745 TO 1772, Emanuel Swedenborg was able to travel between the natural and spiritual worlds
almost daily once his spiritual eyes were open. These experiences
were not simply for his benefit, but also to reveal truths about
the nature of God and the inner meaning of the Bible. It was up
to him to make these revelations available to all who might be
drawn to these insights.

Emanuel Swedenborg was called both *to receive* this information into his understanding and also *to publish* these new
truths by the press. His life was spent in preparation for these
tasks and was influenced by the fortuitous circumstances of his

background—from the family he was born into, to his intelligence, writing skills, scientific preparation, and the opportunities that were available to him. In providence these were provided in preparation of the mission he was called to fulfill.

In his work *Spiritual Diary*, he realized his whole life had been in preparation for this work. He stated:

> I could see at last that the tenor of the Divine providence
> has ruled the acts of my life from my very youth, that I
> might at last come to this end; so that, by means of the
> knowledges of natural things I might be able to understand
> the things which lie deeply concealed in the Word of God,
> and thus serve as an instrument for laying them bare.

The fact that he was chosen to receive this new revelation is well documented in his *Spiritual Diary* and in other writings. The second part of his call—to publish by the press—opened the door to share these insights with others. Through his enlightened writing he was able to fulfill the call that he received—that of receiving new understanding and publishing books that would share it with others. One without the other would not have fulfilled the mission for which he was chosen.

Swedenborg discusses this mission in response to a letter written to him on August 2, 1769, by Reverend Thomas Hartley in which Swedenborg talks about an incident that happened in 1743. He was addressing a concern Hartley expressed about having adequate information about Swedenborg in order to defend Swedenborg's reputation against possible slanderers. Swedenborg relates the circumstances of his birth, family, education, and professional experiences, and concludes:

> But all that I have thus far related, I consider of comparatively little importance; for it is far exceeded by the circum-

stance, that I have been called to a holy office by the Lord himself, who most mercifully appeared before me, His servant, in the year 1743; when he opened my sight into the spiritual world, and granted me to speak with spirits and angels, in which state I have continued up to the present day. From that time I began to print and publish the various arcana that were seen by me and revealed to me, as the arcana concerning Heaven and Hell, the state of man after death, the true worship of God, the spiritual sense of the Word, besides many other most important matters conducive to salvation and wisdom. The only reason of my journeys abroad has been the desire of making myself useful, and of making known the arcana that were entrusted to me. (Tafel, *Documents*)

He went on to explain in another letter in 1771 to Landgrave of Hesse-Darmstadt why it was necessary for God to choose a person to receive the doctrine of a new church:

> But as he cannot come again into the world in person,
> it was necessary that he should do it by means of a man,
> who should not only receive the doctrine of that church by
> his understanding, but also publish it by means of the press;
> and as the Lord had prepared me for this from my child-
> hood, he manifested himself in person before me, his
> servant, and sent me to do this work. This took place in the
> year 1743; and afterwards he opened the sight of my spirit
> and thus introduced me into the spiritual world.
>
> (Tafel, *Documents*)

How Emanuel Swedenborg accomplished this mission is a fascinating tale of trips to London and Amsterdam, locations se-lected for publishing his books. These countries allowed freedom of speech and the press at a time that both Sweden and Germany did not. Thus he was able to publish by going to London and Amsterdam to follow the books through the printing process. Following is an overview of the theological books he published:

1749-1756

The first books that are considered part of the theological writings are the eight volumes of *Arcana Coelestia* written between 1747 and 1753. This extensive work reveals the spiritual sense or inner meaning of the books of Genesis and Exodus.

The books were published during the period of 1749-1757 in London in Latin only, except for volume 2 that was also translated into English. They were brought out anonymously, a continuation of Swedenborg's tradition of publishing some of his scientific and philosophical works anonymously. He published across such a wide array of fields that perhaps:

the veiled approach may have been due to modesty, embarrassment at having overstepped the bounds of his profession. Or it may have come from his desire to avoid being disturbed by possible criticism. . . . So the beginning of each literary cycle was unidentified with any preceding one, as if to give the ideas he propounded a fair chance of acceptance on their own merits, unbiased and unimpressed by preconceived opinions, and freed from the weight of his personality. (Sigstedt, *Swedenborg Epic*)

Publishing the theological volumes anonymously continued until 1767 when *Conjugial Love* was printed in Amsterdam under his own name.

1758

After publishing the full eight volumes of *Arcana Coelestia*, he brought out five derivative works in 1758. *Earths in the Universe* was the first and detailed Swedenbog's conversations in the spiritual world with former inhabitants of other planets. The next book was *Heaven and Hell*, again published in London, as were all five published that year. This volume brought together much of the material related to the first twenty-one chapters from Genesis that was discussed in the *Arcana Coelestia*. It was reordered and arranged to deal with the different levels of heaven and hell, the world of spirits, angels, and the spiritual world. *The Last Judgment* was revolutionary in its announcement that the Last Judgment had already taken place in the spiritual world. *The New Jerusalem and Its Heavenly Doctrine,* which came next, draws from the earlier discussions of Exodus from the *Arcana Coelestia*. *The White Horse,* whose title refers to a white horse in the book of Revelation, primarily focuses on the inner meaning of the Bible and lists the books in the Bible that have a spiritual sense.

Three of these books—*Heaven and Hell, The New Jerusalem and its Heavenly Doctrine*, and *White Horse*—are distillations and new representations of material from the earlier volumes of

Arcana Coelestia, perhaps as an attempt to glean out the important elements for the reader in order to make these ideas more accessible.

1763

The books published in 1763—seven in all—were introduced in the first one, *Doctrine of the Lord*. The next three were *Doctrine of Sacred Scripture, Doctine of Life,* and *Doctrine of Faith.* Next came *Continuation of the Last Judgment,* a work that continued the commentary on the effect the Last Judgment had on the state of the world and the church. This was followed by *Divine Love and Wisdom*, which deals with the story of Creation, and then *Divine Providence,* which identifies the spiritual laws under which we operate. All of the books published in 1763 were printed in Amsterdam in Latin and were still published anonymously.

Five books were published over the next five years, beginning with *Apocalypse Revealed* in 1766. This book provides a detailed explanation of the inner meaning of the book of Revelation and was published in Amsterdam, the last work to appear without Swedenborg's name. Two years later in 1768, again in Amsterdam, *Conjugial Love* was released, this time with Swedenborg's name on the title page and a listing of his other theological works in the back.

In 1769, in London, *A Brief Exposition of the Doctrine of the New Church* was published in Latin as well as English, one of only three books published in English during his lifetime. The first was volume 2 of the *Arcana,* mentioned earlier and translated by John Marchant. *A Brief Exposition* was the second, and translated by the same person. One possible reason to translate the latter book into English was that Swedenborg wanted to distribute copies to professors of theology in England and wanted to make the information more accessible to them.

Next *Soul-Body Interaction* was published in London, first in Latin in 1769, then the following year in English. This time the book was translated by Thomas Hartley and there are indications that this book was not sold commercially, but distributed as a private edition. Some copies were sent to scientific societies in England and France.

Swedenborg's last book was *True Christian Religion*, printed in Amsterdam in 1771 in Latin only. It is his definitive work on the theology of a new church.

The Spritual Diary

While Swedenborg was writing and explaining the new concepts, simultaneously he was also keeping a spiritual diary that would be published posthumously. This diary was written from 1747—

the same year he started the *Arcana Coelestia*—to 1765, after he finished *Divine Providence*. Some of this material reappears in works that were published later, from 1766 to 1771, in sections within the books called *memorable relations*.

After his last work *True Christian Religion* was published in Amsterdam in 1771, he returned to London, suffered a stroke, and passed into the spiritual world in 1772.

Swedenborg provided the bridge between heaven and earth through the revelation he received from his experiences in the spiritual world and by understanding the spiritual sense of the Bible. Part of his mission of receiving these essential truths was the absolute necessity to publish them, so that people could have access to this important information.

The writings of Swedenborg became the vehicle to bring essential insights to a world that needed to receive the news of the internal, or spiritual, sense of the Bible. With this information came greater knowledge of the spiritual dimension within each person as well as steps toward regeneration.

His publications offer an amazing testimony of revelation from the heavens, written in the hand of one who saw and heard. This was made possible by the technology available to publish by the press:

> Of course we would have had no Swedenborg without
> the printing press and the sciences it fostered and made
> available. . . . The modern sciences are his vocabulary; the
> printing press his megaphone (Eby, *The Story of the
> Swedenborg Manuscripts*).

The publishing process was an essential aspect of Swedenborg's work, of the mission he was called to do on this earth. Not only was he prepared personally for this task, but the fortuitous invention in 1454 of the printing press to promulgate the information was important as well.

Swedenborg's two-fold call, which included receiving and publishing his insights, was not an arbitrary one. Publishing became and continues to be the vehicle for bringing awareness to all who can understand the esoteric wisdom contained within the volumes that Swedenborg wrote.

WORKS CITED

Eby, S.C. *The Story of the Swedenborg Manuscripts*. New York: New Church Press, 1926.

Sigstedt, Cyriel Odhner. *The Swedenborg Epic: The Life and Works of Emanuel Swedenborg*. London: The Swedenborg Society, 1981.

Swedenborg, Emanuel. *Swedenborg's Diary: Recounting Spiritual Experiences during the Years 1745 to 1765*. Translated by J. Durban Odhner. Bryn Athyn, PA: General Church of the New Jerusalem, 1998-2002.

Tafel, R.L. *Documents Concerning the Life and Character of Emanuel Swedenborg,* Volumes I and II. London: Swedenborg Society, 1877.

Swedenborg's Theological Works Published 1749-1771

WRITTEN	TITLE	PUBLISHED	WHERE	LANG
1747-53	Arcana Coelestia (8 volumes)	1749-56	London	Latin
	Volume 2 (transl. Marchant)		London	English
1758	Earths in the Universe	1758	London	Latin
1758	Heaven & Hell	1758	London	Latin
1758	Last Judgment	1758	London	Latin
1758	The New Jerusalem and Its Heavenly Doctrine	1758	London	Latin
1758	White Horse	1758	London	Latin
1763	Doctrine of the Lord	1763	Amsterdam	Latin
1763	Doctrine of the Sacred Scripture	1763	Amsterdam	Latin
1763	Doctrine of Life	1763	Amsterdam	Latin
1763	Doctrine of Faith	1763	Amsterdam	Latin
1763	Continuation of the Last Judgment	1763	Amsterdam	Latin
1763	Divine Love and Wisdom	1763	Amsterdam	Latin
1763	Divine Providence	1764	Amsterdam	Latin
1766	Apocalypse Revealed	1766	Amsterdam	Latin
1767	Conjugial Love	1768	Amsterdam	Latin
1769	Brief Exposition of the Doctrine of the New Church	1769	Amsterdam	Latin
	English translation (transl. Marchant)	1769	London	English
1769	Soul-Body Interaction	1769	London	Latin
	English translation (trans. Hartley)	1770	London	English
1771	True Christian Religion	1771	Amsterdam	Latin

 Further Reading

THEOLOGICAL WRITINGS OF EMANUEL SWEDENBORG

There are many translations of the original work *Divine Providence* by Emanuel Swedenborg. Here are three sources and four versions that have been published; these organizations also have available translations of Swedenborg's other works.

Swedenborg, Emanuel. *Angelic Wisdom about Divine Providence.* Translated by George F. Dole. West Chester, PA: Swedenborg Foundation, 2003.

Swedenborg, Emanuel. *Angelic Wisdom regarding Divine Providence.* Translated by N. Bruce Rogers. Bryn Athyn, PA: General Church of the New Jerusalem, 2003.

Swedenborg, Emanuel. *Angelic Wisdom concerning Divine Providence.* Translated by William F. Wunsch. West Chester, PA: Swedenborg Foundation, 1996.

Swedenborg, Emanuel. *Divine Providence.* Translated by William Dick and E. Pulsford. London: The Swedenborg Society, 1988.

RECOMMENDED BIOGRAPHIES

Benz, Ernst. *Emanuel Swedenborg: A Visionary Savant in the Age of Reason*. Translated by Nicholas Goodrick-Clarke. West Chester, PA: Swedenborg Foundation, 2008.

Lamm, Martin. *Emanuel Swedenborg: The Deveopment of His Thought*. Translated by Tomas Spiers and Anders Hallengren. West Chester, PA: Swedenborg Foundation, 2000.

Sigstedt, Cyriel Odhner. *The Swedenborg Epic: The Life and Works of Emanuel Swedenborg*. London: The Swedenborg Society, 1981.

Toksvig, Signe. *Emanuel Swedenborg: Scientist and Mystic*. New York: Swedenborg Foundation, 1983.

Trobridge, George. *Swedenborg: Life and Teaching*. New York: Swedenborg Foundation, 1992.

REFERENCE WORKS

Brock, Erland. *Swedenborg and His Influence*. Bryn Athyn, PA: Swedenborg Scientific Association, 1996.

Larson, Robin. *Emanuel Swedenborg: A Continuing Vision*. New York: Swedenborg Foundation, 1988.

Woofenden, William Ross. *Swedenborg Explorer's Guidebook: A Research Manual*. West Chester, PA: Swedenborg Foundation, 2006.

Bertucci, Mary Lou, and Joanna Hill. *Tiffany's Swedenborgian Angels: Stained Glass Windows Representing the Seven Churches from the Book of Revelation*. West Chester, PA: Swedenborg Foundation, 2011.

Corbin, Henri. *Swedenborg and Esoteric Islam*. West Chester, PA: Swedenborg Foundation, 1995.

Keller, Helen. *How I Would Help the World*. Edited by Ray Silverman. West Chester, PA: Swedenborg Foundation, 2011.

—— *Light in My Darkness*. Edited by Ray Silverman. West Chester, PA: Swedenborg Foundation, 2000.

Lachman, Gary. *Swedenborg: An Introduction to His Life and Ideas*. New York: Tarcher, 2012.

Silverman, Ray. *The Core of Johnny Appleseed: The Unknown Story of a Spiritual Trailblazer*. West Chester, PA: Swedenborg Foundation, 2012.

Suzuki, D.T. *Swedenborg: Buddha of the North*. West Chester, PA: Swedenborg Foundation, 1996.

🌿 Acknowledgements

Many thanks go to Eric Carswell, my thesis advisor, who supported me in this endeavor. Deep gratitude to our home church group led by Roslyn Taylor, who kept Swedenborg alive for me; to my yoga teachers, Rachel Odhner, Lisa Wulf, and Mary Ann Bennett who have helped me stay connected and open; my dear friend and business partner, Marcy Heller, whose support has been immeasurable. And to the ancestors, Aunt Phoebe and Aunt Marjorie, who protected and guided me, and still do.